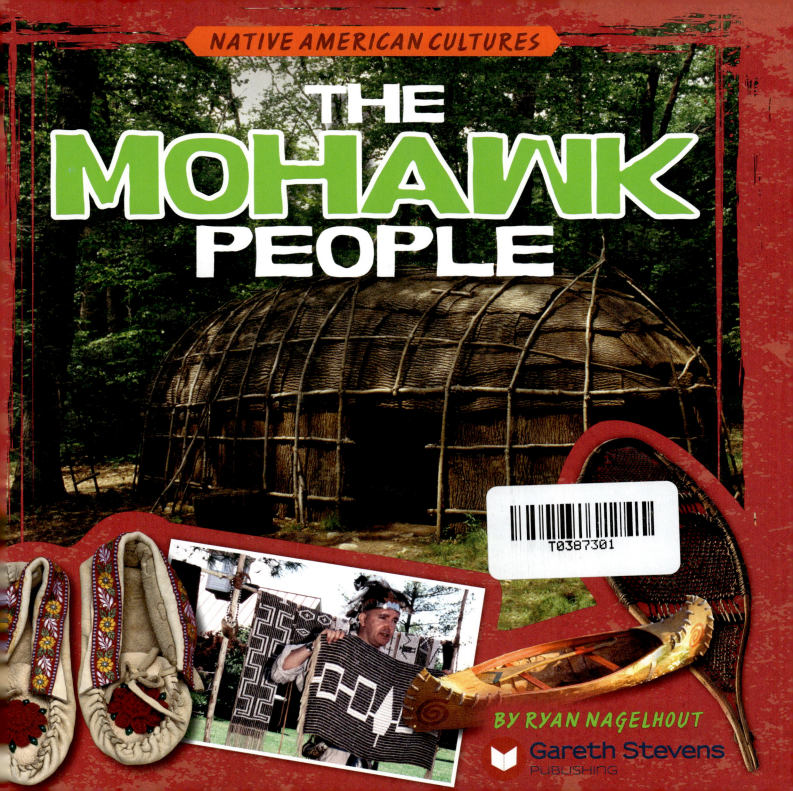

Please visit our website, www.garethstevens.com. For a free color catalog of all our high-quality books, call toll free 1-800-542-2595 or fax 1-877-542-2596.

Library of Congress Cataloging-in-Publication Data

Nagelhout, Ryan.
The Mohawk people / by Ryan Nagelhout.
p. cm. — (Native American cultures)
Includes index.
ISBN 978-1-4824-1990-0 (pbk.)
ISBN 978-1-4824-1989-4 (6-pack)
ISBN 978-1-4824-1991-7 (library binding)
1. Mohawk Indians — Juvenile literature. 2. Mohawk Indians — Social life and customs — Juvenile literature. 3. Mohawk Indians — History — Juvenile literature. 4. Indians of North America — New York (State) — Juvenile literature.I. Nagelhout, Ryan. II. Title.
E99.M8 N34 2015
974.7004—d23

Published in 2015 by
Gareth Stevens Publishing
111 East 14th Street, Suite 349
New York, NY 10003

Copyright © 2015 Gareth Stevens Publishing

Designer: Sarah Liddell
Editor: Therese Shea

Photo credits: Cover, pp. 1 (main image, moccasins, canoe, and snowshoes), 6 Marilyn Angel Wynn/ Nativestock/Getty Images; cover, p. 1 (wampum belt) Education Images/Contributor/Universal Images Group/Getty Images; p. 4 Ævar Arnfjörð Bjarmason/Wikimedia Commons; pp. 5, 13, 29 Jeangagnon/ Wikimedia Commons; p. 7 Stock Montage/Contributor/Archive Photos/Getty Images; p. 8 Alkari/ Wikimedia Commons; pp. 9, 23 (map), 24 Rainer Lesniewski/Shutterstock.com; p. 11 © iStockphoto. com/ecliff6; p. 12 IvoShandor/Wikimedia Commons; p. 15 photo courtesy of the Library of Congress/ W.S. Tanner; p. 17 Harryzilber/Wikimedia Commons; p. 19 (William Johnson) Igrimm12/ Wikimedia Commons; p. 19 (King Hendrick) Kevin Myers/Wikimedia Commons; p. 20 Botaurus/ Wikimedia Commons; p. 21 PhotoQuest/Contributor/Archive Photos/Getty Images; p. 23 (George Washington) Victorian Traditions/Shutterstock.com; p. 25 Bernard Weil/Contributor/Toronto Star/ Getty Images; p. 27 Ray Ellis/Photo Researchers/Getty Images.

All rights reserved. No part of this book may be reproduced in any form without permission in writing from the publisher, except by a reviewer.

Printed in the United States of America

CPSIA compliance information: Batch #CW15GS: For further information contact Gareth Stevens, New York, New York at 1-800-542-2595.

CONTENTS

People of the Flint 4

Longhouse People 6

The Confederacy 8

Life with the Mohawk 10

Mohawk Clothing 12

Speaking the Language 14

Opening the Door 16

Breaking Treaties 18

Picking a Side 20

Destruction 22

Getting Pushed Out 24

Fearless Mohawk 26

Mohawk Today 28

Glossary 30

For More Information 31

Index 32

Words in the glossary appear in **bold** type the first time they are used in the text.

PEOPLE OF THE FLINT

The Mohawk people are a group of Native Americans who live mostly in the northeastern United States and southern Canada. Called the "keepers of the eastern door," they're the easternmost peoples of a famous group of tribes called the Iroquois **Confederacy**.

The first peoples in North America came from eastern Asia about 12,000 years ago. They probably traveled over a land bridge between the two continents. This area is now the Bering Strait, which runs between Russia and Alaska.

BERING STRAIT

RUSSIA

ALASKA

DID YOU KNOW?

"Mohawk" means "cowards" in the language of the Abenaki people, enemies of the Mohawk.

The Mohawk people call themselves *kanien'keha:ka* (gan-yun-GEH-ha-ga), which means "people of the flint." Flint is a hard, gray-black rock that was found in their territory.

LONGHOUSE PEOPLE

The Mohawk and other members of the Iroquois Confederacy called themselves Haudenosaunee (HOH-dee-noh-SHOH-nee), which means "people building a longhouse." A longhouse is a home built from wood and bark for several families.

Longhouses were from 40 to 400 feet (12 to 122 m) long and were usually 22 or 23 feet (6.7 or 7 m) wide. Each longhouse was home to families that belonged to the same clan, a group of families related to one another.

DID YOU KNOW?

Fires for cooking were built inside a longhouse. There was a hole in the roof over each fire area to let smoke out.

THE CONFEDERACY

Before European explorers came to North America, the Mohawk often fought with the Oneida, Cayuga, Seneca, and Onondaga tribes. One day a man named the Peacemaker (also called Dekanawidah or Skennenrahawi) convinced the tribes to join together as a confederacy to fight against their common enemy, the Algonquian.

The Mohawk were the first to accept the Peacemaker's "Great Law of Peace," a kind of **constitution**. The other four tribes soon followed. In 1722, another tribe, the Tuscarora, joined the group.

CONFEDERACY FLAG

DID YOU KNOW?
French explorers called the group of tribes the "Iroquois Confederacy," but natives used the term "Haudenosaunee." The British called them the "Six Nations."

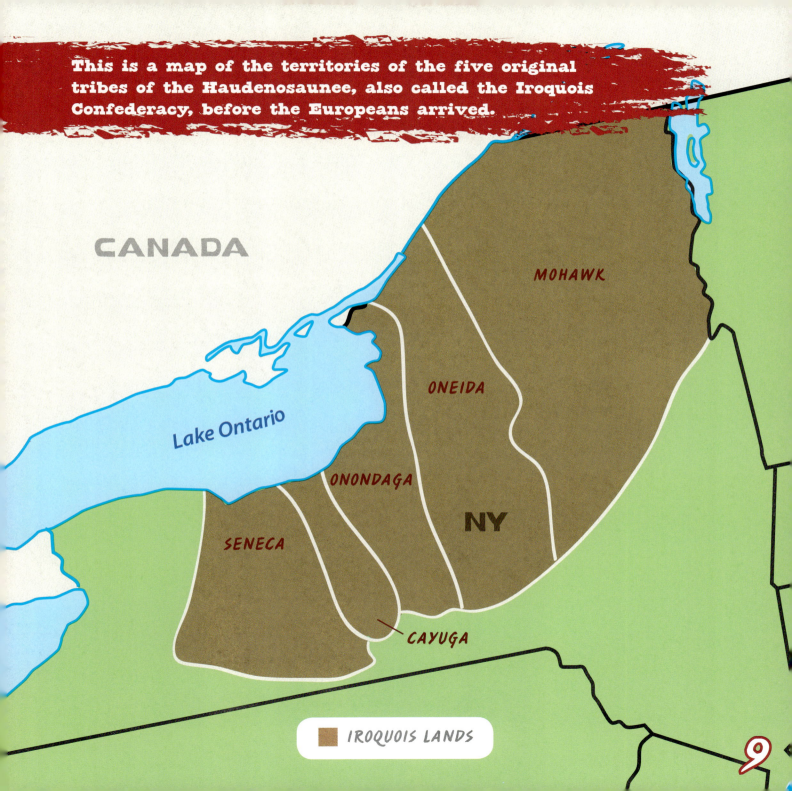

LIFE WITH THE MOHAWK

Traditional Mohawk tribes were matrilineal, which means that all children belonged to their mother's clan. After marriage, a man moved into the longhouse of his wife's clan. Women also owned the family's land and decided what would grow on it. They grew corn, peas, melons, squash, and other crops on their land.

Men hunted, fished, and traded with other tribes. They were also warriors who had to be ready to fight to guard their land and families.

DID YOU KNOW?

Mohawk women grew apple trees and collected syrup from maple trees.

Native youths learned hunting, farming, and other skills from their parents and other relatives.

MOHAWK CLOTHING

Early Mohawk clothing was made out of deerskin. Mohawk men and women wore leggings. Women wore a long dress over them. Shoes called moccasins were often **decorated** with beads and other objects. Men wore feather caps called headdresses during special **ceremonies**. Cloth replaced deerskin clothing for many Mohawk when trade with Europeans began.

In times of war, Mohawk men shaved their heads except for a "scalplock" down the center of their head. This hairstyle is known today as a Mohawk.

MOHAWK

Traditional Mohawk clothing is still worn during special ceremonies.

SPEAKING THE LANGUAGE

The Mohawk language was an oral language, which means it was spoken and not written down. However, it began to be written when European priests came to North America to teach the Mohawk about Christianity. The priests used only 12 letters of the English alphabet: A E H I K N O R S T W Y. They also used these marks: ' and :

She:kon (shay-kohn) is a friendly greeting in the Mohawk language. *Nia:wen* (nee-ah-wenh) means "thank you." Look on the next page to learn more.

DID YOU KNOW?

The Mohawk language is still taught to Mohawk children and can be seen on signs in Mohawk territory.

PRACTICING THE MOHAWK LANGUAGE

KANIEN'KEHA (MOHAWK) WORD	HOW TO SAY IT	MEANS
hen'en	ha-a	yes
yah	e-yah	no
yeksa'ah	yek-saw	girl
raksa'ha	lock-saw	boy

15

OPENING THE DOOR

Because the Mohawk were the easternmost tribe of the confederacy, they were the first Native Americans to meet European explorers. The French first came upon the Mohawk in 1534. The Mohawk met the Dutch in 1609 and the British in 1664.

Early meetings between the Mohawk and European explorers were mostly peaceful. The Mohawk signed a **treaty** with Dutch explorers called the **Covenant** Chain. The Dutch supplied the Mohawk with guns to fight their Algonquian enemies.

DID YOU KNOW?

The Mohawk and other tribes of the confederacy used different colored beads strung together in belts to record their history. These were called wampum belts.

Here, Iroquois chiefs explain the meanings of their wampum belts.

BREAKING TREATIES

The treaties the Mohawk signed with the Dutch and later the British said that each nation was independent and equal with its own lands. However, as more European settlers arrived, they moved onto lands claimed by the Mohawk.

A Mohawk leader named Teoniahigarawe, called King Hendrick by Europeans, met with the British governor of New York, George Clinton, in 1753 about land claims. Clinton refused to honor their treaty and allowed British settlers to stay on Mohawk land. King Hendrick declared that the Covenant Chain was broken.

DID YOU KNOW?

In 1664, the Dutch gave up their North American lands to the British. The British then made treaties with the Mohawk.

KING HENDRICK

WILLIAM JOHNSON

British colonel William Johnson, a friend of King Hendrick, asked to restore the Covenant Chain. However, the British agreed to and broke the Covenant Chain several times.

PICKING A SIDE

The Mohawk played a large role in European wars in North America. Some Mohawk helped the British win their first battle in the French and Indian War (1754–1763). King Hendrick was killed in action. This war would later force France out of much of North America.

Many Mohawk sided with the British during the American Revolution. However, the war between the colonists and the British divided the Iroquois Confederacy. Mohawk leader Joseph Brant—also called Thayendanegea (tai-yen-da-nay-geh)—and his followers supported the British.

JOSEPH BRANT

Four of the Iroquois nations, including the Mohawk, sided with the British during the American Revolution.

DESTRUCTION

During the American Revolution, American general George Washington ordered the destruction of all Iroquois people and territory. Countless Mohawk died as American soldiers killed every man, woman, and child they could find.

The Treaty of Paris, signed in 1783 to end the war, set up a border between the United States and Canada through Mohawk territory. Joseph Brant and many Mohawk fled to Canada, where the British government gave them 1,200 square miles (3,100 sq km) on the Grand River in Ontario.

DID YOU KNOW?

The Mohawk who stayed in the United States signed a treaty at Fort Stanwix in 1784 establishing the borders of their territory.

About 40 Iroquois villages were destroyed. Washington received the name Conotocarious, or "Town Destroyer."

GETTING PUSHED OUT

Mohawk people continued to see their treaties broken as the United States and Canada grew. The Mohawk were pushed off their lands and sent to live on **reservations**. Today, there are several Mohawk reservations in Canada and the United States.

Mohawk people were forced to take on the **culture** of white settlers. They had to wear clothes like those of the whites and practice Christianity. Mohawk children were sent to schools to learn English. They were taught European and American history, but not their own.

MOHAWK RESERVATIONS

CANADA
KAHNAWAKE
KANEHSATAKE
Saint Lawrence R.
WAHTA
Lake Huron
TYENDINAGA
NY
Lake Ontario
AKWESASNE
MI
SIX NATIONS
Lake Erie
PA
UNITED STATES

The Akwesasne reservation lies across the border of the United States and Canada.

FEARLESS MOHAWK

In the 1880s, some Mohawk were found to have a special skill in construction. As a bridge was being built across the St. Lawrence River onto Mohawk land, Mohawk men climbed the highest beams without fear. Since they were unafraid of great heights, the bridge workers hired them to help. Soon, other job opportunities opened up.

Some Mohawk moved to New York City to work on tall buildings, or skyscrapers, being built there. The Mohawk have worked on the Empire State Building, the World Trade Center, and the newly built One World Trade Center.

Historians say nearly every skyscraper in New York City was built by Mohawk and other Native American ironworkers. Some Mohawk traveled long distances from their homes to building sites.

MOHAWK TODAY

Today, the Mohawk people are trying to reclaim some of their historic territory from the United States and Canadian governments. They use treaties made years ago as proof that they weren't treated justly by the governments.

Many Mohawk still live on reservations, but some live in towns and cities throughout southeastern Ontario and the eastern United States. They dress and act as other Americans and Canadians, while working hard to make sure the Mohawk culture doesn't die out.

DID YOU KNOW?

It's thought that about 47,000 Mohawk descendants live in the United States and Canada today.

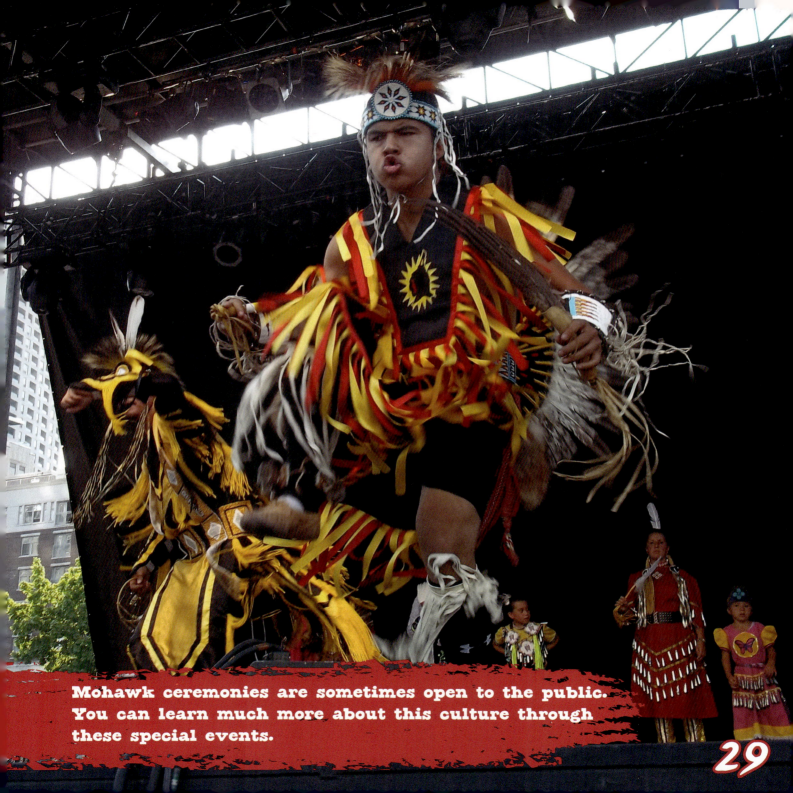

Mohawk ceremonies are sometimes open to the public. You can learn much more about this culture through these special events.

GLOSSARY

ceremony: an event to honor or celebrate something

confederacy: a group of people or states joined in a common purpose

constitution: the basic laws by which a country or state is governed

covenant: a formal agreement

coward: someone who shows shameful fear

culture: the beliefs and ways of life of a group of people

decorate: to add something to make a piece of clothing look special

descendant: a relative of someone from an earlier time

reservation: land set aside by the government for Native Americans

traditional: having to do with long-practiced customs

treaty: an agreement between countries or peoples

FOR MORE INFORMATION

BOOKS

Crompton, Samuel Willard. *The Mohawk*. New York, NY: Chelsea House Publishers, 2010.

Hinton, Kaavonia. *The Iroquois of the Northeast*. Kennett Square, PA: Purple Toad Publishing, 2013.

King, David C. *The Mohawk*. New York, NY: Marshall Cavendish Benchmark, 2010.

WEBSITES

Mohawk Indian Fact Sheet
bigorrin.org/mohawk_kids.htm
Learn more facts about the Mohawk people on this site.

Mohawk Indian Language
native-languages.org/mohawk.htm
Read about Mohawk language and culture here.

Publisher's note to educators and parents: Our editors have carefully reviewed these websites to ensure that they are suitable for students. Many websites change frequently, however, and we cannot guarantee that a site's future contents will continue to meet our high standards of quality and educational value. Be advised that students should be closely supervised whenever they access the Internet.

INDEX

American Revolution 20, 21, 22

Brant, Joseph 20, 22

British 8, 16, 18, 19, 20, 21, 22

clan 6, 10

clothing 12, 13

Covenant Chain 16, 18, 19

Dutch 16, 18

Europeans 8, 9, 12, 14, 16, 18, 20, 24

French 8, 16

French and Indian War 20

Great Law of Peace 8

Haudenosaunee 6, 8, 9

Hendrick, King 18, 19, 20

Iroquois Confederacy 4, 8, 9, 16, 20

language 14, 15

longhouse 6, 7, 10

men 10, 12

Peacemaker 8

reservations 24, 25, 28

skyscrapers 26, 27

treaties 16, 18, 22, 24, 28

Treaty of Paris 22

wampum belts 16, 17

Washington, George 22, 23

women 10, 12